Topps
MATCH ATTAX

ANNUAL 2020

With 32 wins, 98 points and 95 goals in the bag, Manchester City once again proved they were the best in the Premier League! Check out how they clinched the trophy.

MANCHESTER CITY

TEAM TALK

With probably the strongest squad in the league, boss Pep Guardiola had plenty of options to keep Manchester City in the title race. Aguero and Jesus were his main strikers, with Sterling in support, and Sane, Mahrez and Bernardo Silva operating out wide. De Bruyne struggled with injury but Gundogan got game time and teenager Foden bagged his first league goal.

SEASON STATS

POSITION:	1ST
PREMIER LEAGUE POINTS:	98
PREMIER LEAGUE WINS:	32
PREMIER LEAGUE GOALS SCORED:	95
PREMIER LEAGUE GOALS CONCEDED:	23
CLEAN SHEETS:	20
SHOTS:	683
PENALTIES SCORED:	3
PASSES:	26,581
CROSSES:	783
TACKLES:	518
YELLOW CARDS:	44
RED CARDS:	1
FOULS:	193
OFFSIDES:	98

MEGA MOMENT > > > > >

With time running out and Manchester City fearing they would drop points against Leicester City, captain Vincent Kompany became a superhero at The Etihad! The veteran defender collected the ball in front of The Foxes' goal and struck a sweet long-range effort that rifled past goalkeeper Kasper Schmeichel. Kompany's winner kept the title in reach and sent the crowd crazy!

5 EPIC STARS

SERGIO AGUERO
Aguero did his usual trick of blasting in goals, goals and goals! By May 2019 he had a mighty 164 in just 239 league games. The fans worship him!

FERNANDINHO
The midfield heartbeat, offering defensive protection and a quick brain to start attacks. He linked up superbly with the Silvas, Sane and De Bruyne.

BERNARDO SILVA
A wizard with the ball, Silva caused carnage from the wings as well as through the centre. He recorded 15 goals and assists combined – his best City stats so far!

LEROY SANE
The skilful German didn't always start, but he regularly made a big impact with his goals, assists and speed. His winner against rivals Liverpool FC was class.

EDERSON
With 20 clean sheets and having conceded just 23 goals, Ederson's second season at The Etihad confirmed his world-class talent. He's so confident in possession.

PLAYER OF THE YEAR

RAHEEM STERLING

Sterling enjoyed his finest season as he clinched his second Premier League title with Manchester City. He worked his magic on the pitch, leaving defenders for dust and racing into the box to score or assist his team-mates. He was crowned PFA Young Player of the Year and the Football Writers' Association Player of the Year!

POSITION:	FORWARD
PREMIER LEAGUE GAMES:	34
PREMIER LEAGUE GOALS:	17
PASSES:	1,263
ASSISTS:	10
CROSSES:	75
RIGHT-FOOT GOALS:	11
LEFT-FOOT GOALS:	4
YELLOW CARDS:	3
RED CARDS:	0
FOULS:	40

LIVERPOOL FC

TEAM TALK

Manager Jurgen Klopp had a strong team spine to rely on, with Alisson in goal, Van Dijk in central defence and captain Henderson taking charge of midfield. The Reds' famous front three of Salah, Mane and Firmino dazzled again, grabbing 56 between them in the Premier League. New signings Fabinho and Keita impressed as the season unfolded and even squad players Shaqiri and Origi delivered moments of magic when called into the action.

POSITION:	2ND
PREMIER LEAGUE POINTS:	97
PREMIER LEAGUE WINS:	30
PREMIER LEAGUE GOALS SCORED:	89
PREMIER LEAGUE GOALS CONCEDED:	22
CLEAN SHEETS:	21
SHOTS:	575
PENALTIES SCORED:	7
PASSES:	23,638
CROSSES:	721
TACKLES:	610
YELLOW CARDS:	38
RED CARDS:	2
FOULS:	185
OFFSIDE:	77

MEGA MOMENT > > > > >

The Reds took the title fight to the last game of the season, thanks to a thriller in their second-to-last game at Newcastle United. They were drawing 2–2 with minutes left when substitute striker Divock Origi leapt high in the box to meet a cross and nodded home to snatch an unbelievable win. Sadly Liverpool FC lost the league by a single point, but moments like this will never be forgotten!

ANDREW ROBERTSON
Robertson became one of the best left-backs in the world! The energetic Scotsman made 11 assists, 80 tackles and 30 interceptions. Vital in defence and attack.

SADIO MANE
Mane battled with team-mate Salah to grab the Premier League Golden Boot! He finished with 22, including a crucial injury-time strike against Crystal Palace.

MOHAMED SALAH
Salah shone again, netting 22 and bagging eight assists. By the end of the season his total league record stood at an incredible 56 goals in just 87 appearances!

ALISSON
Signed in summer 2018 for around £66 million, the big Brazilian keeper showed exactly why he's worth that cash! He made superb saves all season and errors were rare.

TRENT ALEXANDER-ARNOLD
Along with Robertson, the youngster was the most eye-catching full-back in 2018–19. He made 12 assists and 201 crosses.

Give me a cape and mask – I'm a superhero defender!

Van Dijk was named the official Premier League **Player of the Season** for 2018–19.

PLAYER OF THE YEAR

VIRGIL VAN DIJK

Liverpool FC fans know the powerful Dutchman is the real leader in their team! In 2018–19 he played every Premier League game, keeping 20 clean sheets as they let in just 22 goals. He's a monster in the air and times tackles to perfection. Van Dijk also notched big goals for The Reds, finding the net against Newcastle United, Watford and Wolves.

POSITION:	DEFENDER
PREMIER LEAGUE GAMES:	38
PREMIER LEAGUE GOALS:	4
PASSES:	3,037
ASSISTS:	2
CLEAN SHEETS:	20
TACKLES:	38
CLEARANCES:	199
YELLOW CARDS:	1
RED CARDS:	0
FOULS:	12

The Blues scrapped for a top-four spot and, even though they weren't at their best, they still beat Manchester City, Arsenal and Tottenham Hotspur!

CHELSEA

TEAM TALK

Chelsea stuck to a 4-3-3 formation with the likes of Gonzalo Higuain, Eden Hazard and Olivier Giroud spearheading the attack at times. N'Golo Kante played in a wider midfield role and Ross Barkley, Callum Hudson-Odoi and Ruben Loftus-Cheek showed signs of their special skills going forwards. Eden Hazard and Willian were the main creative forces.

POSITION: 3RD
PREMIER LEAGUE POINTS: 72
PREMIER LEAGUE WINS: 21
PREMIER LEAGUE GOALS SCORED: 63
PREMIER LEAGUE GOALS CONCEDED: 39
CLEAN SHEETS: 16
SHOTS: 607
PENALTIES SCORED: 5
PASSES: 25,070
CROSSES: 692
TACKLES: 618
YELLOW CARDS: 49
RED CARDS: 0
FOULS: 169
OFFSIDES: 83

MEGA MOMENT > > > > >

Chelsea began 2018-19 in fantastic form, winning their first five league games and going unbeaten in 12. In early December they defeated Manchester City 2-0 at Stamford Bridge, with N'Golo Kante and David Luiz hitting the net. It was Chelsea manager Maurizio Sarri's first victory over Pep Guardiola and The Blues' fans absolutely loved causing Manchester City's first league loss of the season!

5 EPIC STARS

WILLIAN
The tricky Brazilian took his league total for goals and assists at Chelsea to more than 50. He's full of flicks, turns, dribbles and fierce long-range strikes.

PEDRO
The Spanish forward chipped in with big goals in big games throughout 2018-19, netting in important wins over London rivals Tottenham Hotspur and Arsenal.

GONZALO HIGUAIN
A goal machine around Europe, Higuain joined on loan from AC Milan and blasted a debut double against Huddersfield Town. Helped make Chelsea a threat up top.

DAVID LUIZ
Luiz won back his spot in defence after a disappointing spell in 2017-18. The Brazilian helped to keep 15 clean sheets and had a 76 per cent tackle success rate.

KEPA ARRIZABALAGA
After joining from Athletic Bilbao for a world-record £71 million, Kepa made 14 clean sheets in the league and 82 saves. He'll be stronger still in his second season!

> **Hazard** spent seven seasons at Stamford Bridge before a mega-money move to **Real Madrid** in the summer.

PLAYER OF THE YEAR

EDEN HAZARD

The brilliant Belgian was once again the star man at Stamford Bridge, clocking up more goals and assists than any of his teammates. Hazard was awesome with the ball at his feet and dribbled, flicked and dazzled his way past defenders into the box. He grabbed seven goals in six games as Chelsea enjoyed a quick-fire start to the season.

POSITION:	FORWARD
PREMIER LEAGUE GAMES:	37
PREMIER LEAGUE GOALS:	16
PASSES:	1,819
ASSISTS:	15
CROSSES:	145
RIGHT-FOOT GOALS:	11
LEFT-FOOT GOALS:	5
YELLOW CARDS:	2
RED CARDS:	0
FOULS:	12

BOOT THE NET!

Arsenal ace **Alexandre Lacazette** collected 27 goals and 12 assists in his first 67 league games for The Gunners!

```
                                                    C   N   L
                                                        D   Z
                                        R   T   H   H   D   O
                                            H   Y   D   D   W
                                            X   X   B   C   Y
                                        L   Z   Z   B   N   D
W  S  Z  A  C  E  W  X  E  Y  C  I  T  H  D  E
J  B  T  D  F  I  Z  N  M  I  T  H  H  D  Z
F  E  O  E  L  A  A  V  R  H  E  H  O
B  R  S  S  R  M  Y  E  N  E  X  D  W
C  W  O  U  G  L  J  S  A  T  X  B  Y
J  N  W  J  S  O  I  A  L  Z  B  C  D
K  U  Q  H  V  E  U  N  F  G  Q  R  R
U  X  T  I  I  G  T  N  D  X  A  X  A
V  U  L  H  M  C  J  E  W  E  Y  C  V
V  I  C  F  P  A  W  R  Y  E  W  P  C
M  C  S  O  N  H  X  S  T  S  W  I  G
Y  H  D  C  D  B  Y  O  G  A  P  D  W
A  D  Y  B  S  O  L  N  W  S  R  L  S
R  I  C  H  A  R  L  I  S  O  N  L  P
H  A  S  P  E  W  Y  U  W  E  F  T  Z
```

Spot these red-hot Premier League goal-grabbers stuffed inside the boot!

MANE
STERLING
SON
WILSON
ANDERSON
JESUS
DEENEY
VARDY
MILIVOJEVIC

RICHARLISON
MURRAY
WILLIAN
LACAZETTE
FIRMINO
MARTIAL
MOURA
JIMENEZ

> Yep. I'm the Mane man at Anfield!

Liverpool FC star **Sadio Mane** finished the 2018–19 season as the Premier League's joint top scorer with 22 goals.

```
W   S   Z
S   B   Z   D
F   U   O   E   L
Y   A   R   R   U   M
E   V   L   Q   F   M   V   N   X   O
P   T   R   R   O   H   J   A   N   L   C   M
A   G   T   U   U   O   O   I   M   T   B   U   J
I   R   R   E   D   V   M   L   M   E   T   X   J
A   A   H   M   Z   R   J   L   U   E   U   R   S
N   X   X   F   I   A   R   I   R   I   N   B   F
F   P   Y   F   H   M   C   W   O   W   M   E   I
X   M   V   W   B   D   U   A   O   I   O   I   Z
M   A   R   T   I   A   L   S   L   T   A   Z   V
N   M   E   O   N   B   A   U   Z   Q   A   X   L
X   J   L   F   P   H   V   V   W   R   N   Q   Z
```

ANSWERS ON PAGE 79.

TOTTENHAM HOTSPUR

TEAM TALK

With Alderweireld and Vertonghen one of the best defensive duos in the league, boss Mauricio Pochettino could use Winks and Sissoko as midfield protection. That allowed creative heroes like Eriksen, Moura, Dele Alli and Lamela to set up chances for Kane and Son. Trippier was a handy attacking outlet from full-back down the right wing.

SEASON STATS

POSITION:	4TH
PREMIER LEAGUE POINTS:	71
PREMIER LEAGUE WINS:	23
PREMIER LEAGUE GOALS SCORED:	67
PREMIER LEAGUE GOALS CONCEDED:	39
CLEAN SHEETS:	13
SHOTS:	537
PENALTIES SCORED:	4
PASSES:	21,295
CROSSES:	643
TACKLES:	626
YELLOW CARDS:	56
RED CARDS:	3
FOULS:	225
OFFSIDES:	74

MEGA MOMENT >>>>>

Tottenham Hotspur smashed Everton for six away from home, but their best away display was a 3–0 win at Manchester United. The Londoners outclassed The Red Devils and two quick goals from Kane and Moura at the start of the second half set them up. Moura's second strike late on gave Spurs their third win in a row as they made an early-season title charge.

5 EPIC STARS

HEUNG-MIN SON
Son has reached double figures for goals in the last three seasons for Spurs. The fearsome South Korea forward also struck six assists in 2018–19!

CHRISTIAN ERIKSEN
Spurs are much more dangerous when Eriksen is in the side. The Dane's dribbling, speed, set pieces and long-range shooting are totally top class!

TOBY ALDERWEIRELD
The powerful defender kept 12 clean sheets as the focus of Spurs' defence. In 2018–19 he only missed four matches and had a 65 per cent tackle success.

LUCAS MOURA
In his first full season for Tottenham Hotspur, the Brazil midfielder displayed his sweet skills and ability to race into the box. Played wide and central.

DELE ALLI
The England ace was hit by injuries, but he still tapped in five goals and was a vital link player for the strikers. Scored in big wins over Chelsea and Everton.

Watch out – there's a Hurri-Kane blowing in!

Kane scooped the famous FIFA World Cup Golden Boot trophy as the top scorer in 2018 with **six goals** for England.

PLAYER OF THE YEAR

HARRY KANE

Kane's attacking stats are as good as ever! In his 28 league games last season, he netted 17 goals before injury ended his season. He made four assists and had 46 shots on target. In 2018–19 the England captain never went more than three Premier League games without scoring and netted against Manchester United, Arsenal and Chelsea.

POSITION:	FORWARD
PREMIER LEAGUE GAMES:	28
PREMIER LEAGUE GOALS:	17
PASSES:	551
ASSISTS:	4
CROSSES:	12
RIGHT-FOOT GOALS:	12
LEFT-FOOT GOALS:	3
YELLOW CARDS:	5
RED CARDS:	0
FOULS:	31

ARSENAL

Erm. are we shooting this way?

TEAM TALK

Arsenal lost their first two league fixtures, but then went on a run of 14 games without defeat. Kolasinac and Monreal battled for the left-back role with Sokratis, Mustafi or Koscielny taking up the two centre-back spots in a flat back four. Lacazette and Aubameyang often started together with Mkhitaryan, Iwobi and Ramsey threading forward passes.

SEASON STATS

POSITION: 5TH
PREMIER LEAGUE POINTS: 70
PREMIER LEAGUE WINS: 21
PREMIER LEAGUE GOALS SCORED: 73
PREMIER LEAGUE GOALS CONCEDED: 51
CLEAN SHEETS: 8
SHOTS: 467
PENALTIES SCORED: 4
PASSES: 20,805
CROSSES: 605
TACKLES: 609
YELLOW CARDS: 72
RED CARDS: 2
FOULS: 227
OFFSIDES: 89

MEGA MOMENT

During Arsenal's 14-game unbeaten league run, they smashed north-London rivals Spurs 4–2 at The Emirates. An Aubameyang double, plus finishes from Lacazette and Torreira, secured the three points. Arsenal also enjoyed a sweet 2–0 win over Chelsea in January, but beating Tottenham Hotspur is always top of a Gunners fan's wishlist!

5 EPIC STARS

ALEXANDRE LACAZETTE
The Frenchman was often used as part of a two-man attack, with Aubameyang playing just behind. His coolness in the box was impressive.

HENRIKH MKHITARYAN
Mkhitaryan outshone Ozil to clock up ten goals and assists in total. His sharp brain and precise passing gave the forwards ammunition.

MATTEO GUENDOUZI
Guendouzi proved to be a £7 million bargain, playing 33 games and tackling and pressing hard in front of his defence. Needs to add goals to his game now.

SOKRATIS
He became The Gunners' top centre-back, clocking five clean sheets with 108 clearances and 26 interceptions. He was missed when he was injured in late January.

HECTOR BELLERIN
Arsenal's first-choice right-back reached 143 league appearances and chipped in with five assists and 785 passes. Bursting with speed and well-timed tackles!

Aubameyang and **Mkhitaryan** are a sharp mix for Arsenal. They first starred together playing for **Borussia Dortmund** in Germany!

PLAYER OF THE YEAR

PIERRE-EMERICK AUBAMEYANG

The super striker jointly won the Golden Boot in 2018–19 with 22 goals. In his first 49 league games for Arsenal, he bagged 32 goals and nine assists. Aubameyang was Player of the Month in October and his skillled strikes with his right, left and from the penalty spot makes him a deadly finisher. Linking up with Lacazette and Mkhitaryan gives Arsenal the firepower to make defenders weep!

POSITION:	FORWARD
PREMIER LEAGUE GAMES:	36
PREMIER LEAGUE GOALS:	22
PASSES:	692
ASSISTS:	5
CROSSES:	43
RIGHT-FOOT GOALS:	20
LEFT-FOOT GOALS:	2
YELLOW CARDS:	0
RED CARDS:	0
FOULS:	13

MANCHESTER UNITED

TEAM TALK

When Ole Gunnar Solskjaer took charge in December 2018, Manchester United won their next six league games to rocket up the table. Solskjaer got the team playing quick, attractive footy with plenty of goals and chances being created. They used a back four and three forwards, with Pogba bossing the midfield and the full-backs pressing down the wings.

SEASON STATS

POSITION:	6TH
PREMIER LEAGUE POINTS:	66
PREMIER LEAGUE WINS:	19
PREMIER LEAGUE GOALS SCORED:	65
PREMIER LEAGUE GOALS CONCEDED:	54
CLEAN SHEETS:	7
SHOTS:	526
PENALTIES SCORED:	9
PASSES:	19,202
CROSSES:	638
TACKLES:	581
YELLOW CARDS:	73
RED CARDS:	4
FOULS:	221
OFFSIDES:	90

MEGA MOMENT >>

Solskjaer scored 126 goals as a Manchester United player. As soon as he took over from Jose Mourinho, The Red Devils looked like a different team that wanted to get into the box and cause damage. Ole won his first game 5–1 at Cardiff and he didn't lose a Premier League match until a 2–0 defeat to Arsenal in March. Their season faded, but he certainly saved it!

5 EPIC STARS

ANTHONY MARTIAL
The flying France forward hit top gear in October through to December, scoring eight in just ten games. He finished with ten strikes and two assists.

MARCUS RASHFORD
The former youth star edged ahead of Romelu Lukaku in the striking pecking order. Rashford was amazing down the wings, dribbling into the box or leading the line.

LUKE SHAW
Shaw bounced back to show the form that makes him one of the best all-round defenders in the league. Made four assists and 52 crosses into the box.

DAVID DE GEA
The Spain star made over 122 saves and played every Premier League game. He took some criticism, but de Gea's been a big influence at Old Trafford since 2011!

JESSE LINGARD
With his speed, passing, dribbling, long-range shooting and clever assists, Lingard's a hero at Old Trafford. His goal celebrations are pretty special, too!

Pogba went goal crazy when Solskjaer took charge, grabbing four goals in the manager's first three games!

PLAYER OF THE YEAR

PAUL POGBA

The FIFA World Cup winner had a big season at Old Trafford, being directly involved in 22 league goals. He bagged doubles against Huddersfield Town, AFC Bournemouth and Fulham and completed over 2,000 passes and made 28 crosses. He had a quiet end to the season, but when he's in top gear Pogba is one of the best all-action midfielders in world footy!

POSITION:	MIDFIELDER
PREMIER LEAGUE GAMES:	35
PREMIER LEAGUE GOALS:	13
PASSES:	2,068
ASSISTS:	9
CROSSES:	28
RIGHT-FOOT GOALS:	11
LEFT-FOOT GOALS	1
YELLOW CARDS:	6
RED CARDS:	0
FOULS:	54

WOLVERHAMPTON WANDERERS

TEAM TALK

Picking up points against Chelsea, Manchester City, Tottenham Hotspur and Manchester United showed just how good Nuno Espirito Santo's team were in 2018–19. Packed with Portuguese playmakers like Joao Moutinho, Ruben Neves and Diogo Jota, Wolves played an eye-catching passing game. Raul Jimenez was the main striker and Coady and Boly bossed the backline.

SEASON STATS

POSITION: 7TH
PREMIER LEAGUE POINTS: 57
PREMIER LEAGUE WINS: 16
PREMIER LEAGUE GOALS SCORED: 47
PREMIER LEAGUE GOALS CONCEDED: 46
CLEAN SHEETS: 9
SHOTS: 477
PENALTIES SCORED: 4
PASSES: 16,618
CROSSES: 622
TACKLES: 720
YELLOW CARDS: 72
RED CARDS: 1
FOULS: 223
OFFSIDES: 73

MEGA MOMENT >>>>>

Nuno Espirito Santo steered Wolverhampton Wanderers to a memorable 3–1 win against Tottenham Hotspur at Wembley. Wolves were behind with 18 minutes to go before goals from Boly, Jimenez and Costa sealed the shock win. It made the rest of the league really respect the newcomers as a genuine top-ten team, while Jimenez's finish capped a cool team move.

5 EPIC STARS

WILLY BOLY
Goals against Newcastle United, Tottenham Hotspur and Manchester City earned Wolves vital points. Boly was immense in defence and well worth his transfer fee.

JONNY
Wolves snapped up the left-sided star in January 2019 after he joined on loan in the summer from Atletico Madrid. Jonny has quality tackling and passing in his locker!

MATT DOHERTY
One of the best wing-backs of the season, Doherty was involved in nine league goals for Wolves. Speedy, accurate and always a threat from set pieces.

JOAO MOUTINHO
With over 100 Portugal caps, Moutinho has the experience and skills to boss Wolves' midfield. He struck eight assists and netted a big goal at Old Trafford in the league.

DIOGO JOTA
The elegant attacker was at it again in 2018–19, scoring classy strikes against Chelsea and Newcastle United and an epic hat-trick to beat Leicester City!

I'm as hungry as a wolf! Feed me now!

Raul Jimenez was so impressive that in April, Wolves agreed to pay Benfica a club record **£30 million** to sign him permanently!

PLAYER OF THE YEAR

RAUL JIMENEZ

Master Mexico marksman Jimenez scored headers, penalties, tap-ins and power-packed drills for Wolves in 2018–19 while originally on loan from Benfica. The club's top scorer was a nightmare for defenders, and his all-round game impressed fans as he clocked up seven assists and linked up superbly with the midfielders and forwards.

POSITION:	FORWARD
PREMIER LEAGUE GAMES:	38
PREMIER LEAGUE GOALS:	13
PASSES:	1,059
ASSISTS:	7
CROSSES:	27
RIGHT-FOOT GOALS:	9
LEFT-FOOT GOALS:	1
YELLOW CARDS:	4
RED CARDS:	0
FOULS:	42

The Toffees dream of being a top-six team and in 2018–19 they showed signs of the type of footy that could finally bring glory back to Goodison Park!

EVERTON

Not fair! Mum says it's my bedtime!

TEAM TALK

Playing with a lone striker, three supporting forwards, defensive midfielders and a back four, Everton worked hard to deliver exciting and attacking footy for the fans. Idrissa Gueye conducted central midfield, Kurt Zouma and Michael Keane created a strong central defence and left-back Lucas Digne became a big star with his fab free-kicks. Jordan Pickford kept his No.1 spot.

POSITION:	8TH
PREMIER LEAGUE POINTS:	54
PREMIER LEAGUE WINS:	15
PREMIER LEAGUE GOALS SCORED:	54
PREMIER LEAGUE GOALS CONCEDED:	46
CLEAN SHEETS:	14
SHOTS:	498
PENALTIES SCORED:	2
PASSES:	16,494
CROSSES:	814
TACKLES:	700
YELLOW CARDS:	55
RED CARDS:	4
FOULS:	250
OFFSIDES:	69

MEGA MOMENT >>>>>

Everton recorded their biggest win of the season with a 5–1 bashing of Burnley on Boxing Day. Mina, Digne (2), Sigurdsson and Richarlison were on the score sheet as The Toffees dominated the game at Turf Moor. It was the perfect Christmas present for Everton following a heavy defeat by Tottenham Hotspur.

5 EPIC STARS

IDRISSA GUEYE
Gueye was so red-hot that Ligue 1 giants PSG tried to buy him in January! He averaged over 50 passes per game and made more than 140 tackles in total.

GYLFI SIGURDSSON
The cool Iceland hero was full of goals, assists and clever passing in 2018–19. Sigurdsson linked up well with Richarlison in front of him.

MICHAEL KEANE
The England defender clocked up his 100th Premier League game and was manager Marco Silva's No.1 centre-back. Tough in the air, he guarded his area well.

ANDRE GOMES
Signed on loan from Barcelona, Portugal midfielder Gomes became a major attacking threat for Everton. Gomes can ping passes and intercept play with tidy tackles.

LUCAS DIGNE
What a lethal left foot this French defender has! He rescued a point against Watford with a wonderful free-kick and also found the back of the net twice at Burnley.

Richarlison bagged his first strikes for Brazil, too, last season in a 5–0 thumping of El Salvador!

PLAYER OF THE YEAR

RICHARLISON

Richarlison joined Everton in an eye-popping move from Watford that cost around £50 million! The dangerous forward hit the net early on, against Wolverhampton Wanderers and Southampton, and also winners over Leicester City and Brighton & Hove Albion. With pace, power and cool finishing, Richarlison can worry any defence for 90 minutes!

POSITION:	FORWARD
PREMIER LEAGUE GAMES:	35
PREMIER LEAGUE GOALS:	13
PASSES:	793
ASSISTS:	1
CROSSES:	47
RIGHT-FOOT GOALS:	7
LEFT-FOOT GOALS:	4
YELLOW CARDS:	5
RED CARDS:	1
FOULS:	32

HIT OR MISS?

Did these super strikes in the 2018–19 season actually cross the goal line... or not?

1

Eden Hazard fires for Chelsea from a tight angle against Huddersfield Town.

IT WAS A GOAL. ✓

IT WASN'T A GOAL.

2

AFC Bournemouth midfielder, Andrew Surman, shoots from distance against Cardiff.

IT WAS A GOAL.

IT WASN'T A GOAL. ✓

③

Celtic's Jozo Simunovic tries to knock the ball past the St Johnstone keeper.

IT WAS A GOAL.

IT WASN'T A GOAL. ✓

Did Leicester City's Jamie Vardy beat the Burnley defence here?

IT WAS A GOAL.

IT WASN'T A GOAL. ✓

④

⑤

Everton captain Seamus Coleman drills an effort against Brighton & Hove Albion.

IT WAS A GOAL. ✓

IT WASN'T A GOAL.

ANSWERS ON PAGE 79.

COMING SOON:
NEW MATCH ATTAX APP!

TAKE ON YOUR FRIENDS!

Challenge your friends to a Match Attax match, whether you're hanging out together or miles apart! We'll keep track of your head-to-head record to reveal which friend is the ultimate Match Attax champion!

LIVE CARDS

These cards can only be found on the App. Attack and Defence stats will go up and down based on players' performances in real games!

FREE CODE IN EVERY PACK!

FREE TO DOWNLOAD!

Get it on your smartphone now!

WEEKLY TOURNAMENTS

Enter tournaments every week – take on players from all around the world and earn silverware to fill up your trophy cabinet!

HOW TO GET THE APP

You can now get the new Match Attax app to collect, swap and play with thousands of other fans! All you need to do is:

STEP 1: Search for "Match Attax" on your app store.

STEP 2: Download the new Match Attax App.

STEP 3: Scan codes found in Match Attax packets to get free digital cards.

STEP 4: Build your digital team and join the fun!

LEICESTER CITY

TEAM TALK

Brendan Rodgers' 4-1-4-1 system, with lone striker Jamie Vardy supported by the likes of James Maddison, Demarai Gray and Harvey Barnes, had great success. Club captain Wes Morgan, Harry Maguire and Jonny Evans competed for the centre-back spots as Wilfred Ndidi and Nampalys Mendy offered midfield protection. The Foxes' full-backs pushed forwards as they tried to win games using Vardy's counter-attacking pace.

SEASON STATS

POSITION: 9TH
PREMIER LEAGUE POINTS: 52
PREMIER LEAGUE WINS: 15
PREMIER LEAGUE GOALS SCORED: 51
PREMIER LEAGUE GOALS CONCEDED: 48
CLEAN SHEETS: 10
SHOTS: 515
PENALTIES SCORED: 5
PASSES: 17,219
CROSSES: 779
TACKLES: 676
YELLOW CARDS: 57
RED CARDS: 5
FOULS: 210
OFFSIDES: 72

MEGA MOMENT >>>>>

Fresh from a 1–0 win at Stamford Bridge just before Christmas, Leicester City enjoyed another gift of three points at Manchester City on Boxing Day! Despite falling behind, The Foxes fought back for a 2–1 victory, with goals from Marc Albrighton and the impressive Ricardo Pereira. It helped them forget the 5–1 thrashing at The Etihad earlier in 2018!

5 EPIC STARS

RICARDO PEREIRA
The Portugal star is a versatile and exciting full-back who can also play on the wings, using his speed and sharp control to link up with the attackers.

JAMES MADDISON
Costing over £22 million, the skilful forward repaid The Foxes with goals, assists and match-winning displays. Named in the England squad for the first time.

BEN CHILWELL
In 2018–19 the left-back made his England debut and only missed two Premier League games. Chilwell put in over 130 crosses as he attacked down the wing.

HARRY MAGUIRE
As powerful and commanding as ever. Maguire made 31 tackles, five blocks and popped up with three goals, including a late winner at Southampton.

WILFRED NDIDI
It's no surprise that Leicester City gave the Nigerian a huge new six-year deal – he's one of the best defensive midfielders in the Premier League!

In his career, **Jamie Vardy** has won the official Premier League Player of the Season, Goal of the Month and Player of the Month awards!

PLAYER OF THE YEAR

JAMIE VARDY

The Foxes' leading striker once again, scoring 18 goals and making four assists in 2018–19. Vardy took his overall tally to 80 in 176 Premier League games. The former England star began to thrive under Rodgers, bagging six in six games when the boss first took charge in late February. Vardy is still the goal king at the King Power Stadium!

POSITION:	FORWARD
PREMIER LEAGUE GAMES:	34
PREMIER LEAGUE GOALS:	18
PASSES:	416
ASSISTS:	4
CROSSES:	28
RIGHT-FOOT GOALS:	11
LEFT-FOOT GOALS:	4
YELLOW CARDS:	3
RED CARDS:	1
FOULS:	19

WEST HAM UNITED

TEAM TALK

Experienced manager Manuel Pellegrini made tweaks to his formation. He often used Marko Arnautovic as a lone striker, but sometimes Javier Hernandez came in as a supporting forward. Declan Rice and Mark Noble patrolled central midfield, with Felipe Anderson, Robert Snodgrass and Michail Antonio breaking into the box. West Ham United scored more goal than Leicester City, Newcastle United and Burnley.

SEASON STATS

POSITION: 10TH
PREMIER LEAGUE POINTS: 52
PREMIER LEAGUE WINS: 15
PREMIER LEAGUE GOALS SCORED: 52
PREMIER LEAGUE GOALS CONCEDED: 55
CLEAN SHEETS: 7
SHOTS: 441
PENALTIES SCORED: 5
PASSES: 16,358
CROSSES: 630
TACKLES: 723
YELLOW CARDS: 59
RED CARDS: 1
FOULS: 182
OFFSIDES: 72

MEGA MOMENT >>>>>>

West Ham United's 2–0 win at Fulham in December was their fourth in a row in the league. It was nearly five years since the club last matched that run! The Hammers cracked in 11 goals in those games as they began to look at a top-ten finish. Another ace match was their goal-crazy 8–0 League Cup victory over Macclesfield Town!

5 EPIC STARS

DECLAN RICE
The combative midfielder or defender only turned 20 in 2019 and has a big future at the London Stadium. He's brave, clever with the ball and full of energy.

MICHAIL ANTONIO
The versatile midfielder took a while to find his scoring boots. When he did, he struck against Cardiff, Fulham and Liverpool FC to collect precious points.

MARKO ARNAUTOVIC
The big Austrian showed off his strength, skills and finishing. He was involved in 14 league goals and rescued a draw at home to Brighton & Hove Albion.

LUKASZ FABIANSKI
Signed from Swansea City for just £7 million, the former Arsenal stopper was calm between the sticks. Lukasz made 148 saves and kept seven clean sheets.

ISSA DIOP
The £22 million young French defender built an impressive reputation in the heart of defence and helped keep The Hammers well away from relegation.

Filipe **Anderson** really is the golden boy at West Ham United – he won an Olympic gold medal with Brazil in 2016!

First prize in the Silly Face competition, too!

PLAYER OF THE YEAR

FELIPE ANDERSON

West Ham United splashed £36 million on Anderson. He took time to get going at the London Stadium, but his cheeky flicked goal against Manchester United showed his talent. The attacker bagged nine goals, four assists and recorded 25 shots on target. Whether finishing with his right or left, Anderson caused carnage for keepers!

POSITION:	MIDFIELDER
PREMIER LEAGUE GAMES:	36
PREMIER LEAGUE GOALS:	9
PASSES:	1,667
ASSISTS:	4
CROSSES:	121
RIGHT-FOOT GOALS:	6
LEFT-FOOT GOALS:	3
YELLOW CARDS:	3
RED CARDS:	0
FOULS:	27

WATFORD

We had a glove-ly season!

TEAM TALK

After Richarlison left for Everton, Watford shared goals around the team with Deeney, Deulofeu and Pereyra scoring 25 between them. Boss Javi Gracia often kept his team narrow and compact to frustrate the opposition, with a 4–2–2–2 formation much of the time. Deeney chased long balls and skilful midfielders ghosted into the penalty area in support.

SEASON STATS

POSITION:	11TH
PREMIER LEAGUE POINTS:	50
PREMIER LEAGUE WINS:	14
PREMIER LEAGUE GOALS SCORED:	52
PREMIER LEAGUE GOALS CONCEDED:	59
CLEAN SHEETS:	7
SHOTS:	437
PENALTIES SCORED:	1
PASSES:	15,462
CROSSES:	570
TACKLES:	655
YELLOW CARDS:	77
RED CARDS:	4
FOULS:	231
OFFSIDES:	89

MEGA MOMENT > > > > >

Watford fans were in dreamland at the start of 2018–19! A 2–1 win against Tottenham Hotspur was the club's fourth in a row and they sat joint top of the table, ahead of teams like Arsenal and Manchester United. A return to European football looked possible and Watford's style and work-rate were applauded by fans around the league.

5 EPIC STARS

ETIENNE CAPOUE
The Frenchman protected his defence superbly with tackles, clearances and aerial battles. Formed an awesome midfield pairing with Doucoure.

TROY DEENEY
As well as being involved in 14 league goals, plus an FA Cup semi-final winner, the Watford captain worked tirelessly for the team in every game.

BEN FOSTER
Although he turned 36 in 2018–19, Foster reached 300 Premier League games, proving he's still a class act. He made 127 saves and kept seven clean sheets.

ABDOULAYE DOUCOURE
The all-action midfielder was a vital part of Watford's success. The popular Frenchman struck five times and loved to power headed goals into the net!

ROBERTO PEREYRA
The Argentine had his most effective season at Vicarage Road, scoring in wins over Brighton & Hove Albion, Crystal Palace, Wolves and Huddersfield Town.

Deulofeu's hat-trick in February 2019 was Watford's first in the top flight since 1986!

PLAYER OF THE YEAR

GERARD DEULOFEU

The Spaniard's first Premier League hat-trick in a 5–1 win at Cardiff caught the eye, but his displays were top class all season. Deulofeu played in a range of roles and was happy to drift wide, win the ball, cross into the box or drive past defenders. Fans will never forget his heroic goals in the FA Cup semi-final against Wolves!

POSITION:	MIDFIELDER
PREMIER LEAGUE GAMES:	30
PREMIER LEAGUE GOALS:	10
PASSES:	718
ASSISTS:	5
CROSSES:	62
RIGHT-FOOT GOALS:	10
LEFT-FOOT GOALS:	0
YELLOW CARDS:	3
RED CARDS:	0
FOULS:	14

CRYSTAL PALACE

TEAM TALK

Crystal Palace went without a win between 1 October and 1 December. Their well-drilled defence helped them keep a much better goal difference than the likes of AFC Bournemouth, Burnley and Southampton around them in the table. Scott Dann's return after injury in 2019 helped keep them tough at the back and loan signing Michy Batshuayi added fresh firepower and pace.

POSITION: 12TH
PREMIER LEAGUE POINTS: 49
PREMIER LEAGUE WINS: 14
PREMIER LEAGUE GOALS SCORED: 51
PREMIER LEAGUE GOALS CONCEDED: 53
CLEAN SHEETS: 12
SHOTS: 493
PENALTIES SCORED: 10
PASSES: 15,243
CROSSES: 577
TACKLES: 730
YELLOW CARDS: 58
RED CARDS: 2
FOULS: 224
OFFSIDE: 78

MEGA MOMENT >>>>>

Schlupp, Townsend and Milivojevic struck as The Eagles flew away with an amazing 3–2 win at Manchester City. The shock result gave Crystal Palace their first back-to-back victories of the season. They also enjoyed a 3–1 win away at Burnley in March as they moved clear of the relegation spots.

5 EPIC STARS

AARON WAN-BISSAKA The right-back rocked it for The Eagles all season! He was tough in tackles, tidy with his passing and broke forward whenever he got the chance.

LUKA MILIVOJEVIC Crystal Palace's mega captain was on top of his game in 2018–19. Setting up attacks and whipping in crosses, he notched 12 goals and is a penalty ace.

JAMES McARTHUR One of the unsung heroes in Crystal Palace's midfield. The hard-working Scot struck three goals in the league and an impressive six assists.

ANDROS TOWNSEND The eye-catching midfielder showed the form that made him an England star a few years ago. He scored against Chelsea, Manchester City and Liverpool FC.

JAMES TOMKINS Playing with Mamadou Sakho in central defence, Tomkins only missed nine league games and helped The Eagles keep nine clean sheets last season.

In over 170 Premier League appearances, **Zaha** has only ever scored one headed goal!

PLAYER OF THE YEAR

WILFRIED ZAHA

The fancy footwork, dribbling and ace shooting of the Crystal Palace forward made him the man to watch at Selhurst Park. Zaha played wide and supported the strikers, and his goals in 2019 against Southampton, West Ham United, Leicester City and Burnley were vital for The Eagles.

POSITION:	FORWARD
PREMIER LEAGUE GAMES:	34
PREMIER LEAGUE GOALS:	10
PASSES:	1,006
ASSISTS:	5
CROSSES:	37
RIGHT-FOOT GOALS:	8
LEFT-FOOT GOALS:	2
YELLOW CARDS:	8
RED CARDS:	1
FOULS:	44

NEWCASTLE UNITED

TEAM TALK

Newcastle United had a terrible start, not winning any of their first ten league games, but bounced back to become a tough team to crack. Boss Rafa Benitez used both a five- and four-man defence, with Rondon and Perez in attack. Box-to-box midfielder Ki Sung-Yueng had annoying injuries but Senegal star Mohamed Diame was consistent in his defensive midfield role.

SEASON STATS

POSITION: 13TH
PREMIER LEAGUE POINTS: 45
PREMIER LEAGUE WINS: 12
PREMIER LEAGUE GOALS SCORED: 42
PREMIER LEAGUE GOALS CONCEDED: 48
CLEAN SHEETS: 11
SHOTS: 446
PENALTIES SCORED: 1
PASSES: 13,490
CROSSES: 711
TACKLES: 714
YELLOW CARDS: 57
RED CARDS: 2
FOULS: 266
OFFSIDE: 59

MEGA MOMENT >>>>>

The Magpies' win over Manchester City in January was epic, but beating Burnley in November was even more important. It was the club's third win in a row and lifted them to 13th in the table. Ben Mee's own goal and a Ciaran Clark header did the damage in the first half as Newcastle United picked up their first away win of the season.

5 EPIC STARS

JAMAAL LASCELLES
The captain was Newcastle United's rock. Lascelles helped to keep 11 clean sheets, had a 66 per cent tackle success and made 213 clearances.

MATT RITCHIE
Whether playing wing-back or midfield, Ritchie remained one of Newcastle United's creative stars. The Scot made eight assists and scored two goals.

SEAN LONGSTAFF
The midfielder only made his Premier League debut on Boxing Day, but went on to play nine games and scored against Burnley. Calm and composed.

AYOZE PEREZ
Perez was lively in attack all season, having 55 shots and scoring 12 goals. He netted winners against Watford and Leicester City, plus a hat-trick v The Saints!

FABIAN SCHAR
The defender took a while to settle, but his passing, power and knack of scoring means the fans really rate him. His goal against Burnley was a beauty.

I smashed it on loan!

Of the **42** league goals that Newcastle United scored, **Rondon** and **Perez** scored or assisted **32** of them!

PLAYER OF THE YEAR

SALOMON RONDON

Rondon's header against AFC Bournemouth showed the fans what he's all about! He crashed a whipped cross home inside the box and went on to bag 11 league goals in the season, including two headers. It was a great deal when he joined on loan from West Bromwich Albion and his muscly displays up front made The Magpies tough to crack.

POSITION:	FORWARD
PREMIER LEAGUE GAMES:	32
PREMIER LEAGUE GOALS:	11
PASSES:	735
ASSISTS:	7
CROSSES:	14
RIGHT-FOOT GOALS:	5
LEFT-FOOT GOALS:	4
YELLOW CARDS:	1
RED CARDS:	0
FOULS:	22

CAPTAIN TEASERS!

Time to name these Premier League players who all wore the captain's armband in 2018–19. Take a look at the clues if you need a little help!

I didn't 'skip' any questions!

1 ANSWER ....

2 ANSWER ......Koscielny......

3 ANSWER ......Kompany......

4 ANSWER ......Smith......

5 ANSWER ......James milner......

6 ANSWER ......Asputer......

7 ANSWER ......Tom......

8 ANSWER ......Heaton......

1. A devilish defender, I'm young at heart.

2. This French skipper's Gunner get you!

3. This legend doesn't need a Pep talk!

4. Myths Timmo is an anagram of my name!

5. My first name is James!

6. The start of my surname is as easy as A to Z!

7. This great Scot's home is a Cottage!

8. It's cold – put the 'heat on'!

9. I Spur my team on to keep a clean sheet!

10. My fave birds are Magpies!

11. Fancy a game of Simon Says?

12. This skipper shares his name with a supermarket!

13. My name rhymes with Les Borgan!

14. Mark my words – I'll Hammer the ball home!

15. You can call me Double C!

16. My name is a famous jumping move in basketball!

ANSWER ...Lorens... ANSWER ...Lascelles... ANSWER ...Fallis... ANSWER ...Morrison...

ANSWER ...Morgan... ANSWER ...Noble... ANSWER ...Dacoudy... ANSWER ...Dunk...

ANSWERS ON PAGE 79.

AFC BOURNEMOUTH

TEAM TALK

AFC Bournemouth started the season very well, losing just twice in their first ten league games. Callum Wilson and Josh King were one of the most impressive strike duos and Ryan Fraser and David Brooks were cool and creative in midfield. Injuries to Brooks, Wilson and captain Simon Francis hit The Cherries, but signings like Dominic Solanke and Chris Mepham stepped in to help the team.

SEASON STATS

POSITION:	14TH
PREMIER LEAGUE POINTS:	45
PREMIER LEAGUE WINS:	13
PREMIER LEAGUE GOALS SCORED:	56
PREMIER LEAGUE GOALS CONCEDED:	70
CLEAN SHEETS:	10
SHOTS:	446
PENALTIES SCORED:	7
PASSES:	15,943
CROSSES:	613
TACKLES:	526
YELLOW CARDS:	60
RED CARDS:	1
FOULS:	170
OFFSIDE:	57

MEGA MOMENT > > > > >

AFC Bournemouth's 4–0 bashing of Chelsea was one of the best in their history! King's double, plus strikes from Brooks and Charlie Daniels, gave The Blues no chance and sent the home fans wild. The Cherries had less possession and made fewer passes, but getting the ball in the net is what really counted!

5 EPIC STARS

JOSH KING
Even though he went nine games without a goal, the Norway striker still had 12 goals to his name and scored doubles over Watford and Chelsea.

RYAN FRASER
Fraser forcing his way down the wings got the crowd on their feet at the Vitality Stadium! He was happy to shoot with either foot and racked up 14 assists.

DAVID BROOKS
He made the leap from Sheffield United in the Championship to the Premier League look easy. A creative midfielder with a talent for scoring and assisting.

JEFFERSON LERMA
Handled his £25 million price tag very well with a series of sick midfield displays. Lerma won 69 per cent of his tackles and made over 1,500 passes!

STEVE COOK
Clocking up his 300th Cherries appearance, the no-nonsense defender guided his side to eight clean sheets. He scored the winner at West Ham United, too.

Boom! Wicked Wilson strikes again!

Callum **Wilson** also scored on his England debut at Wembley against the USA in 2018.

PLAYER OF THE YEAR

CALLUM WILSON

By the end of the season, the England striker's overall Premier League record was a healthy 33 goals in 91 games. He reached that total with a mixture of right and left-foot strikes, headers and penalties. Wilson also made nine assists and averaged nearly 15 passes per game – he's an all-round team superstar for AFC Bournemouth!

POSITION:	STRIKER
PREMIER LEAGUE GAMES:	30
PREMIER LEAGUE GOALS:	14
PASSES:	440
ASSISTS:	9
CROSSES:	20
RIGHT-FOOT GOALS:	7
LEFT-FOOT GOALS:	3
YELLOW CARDS:	3
RED CARDS:	0
FOULS:	41

BURNLEY

TEAM TALK

Manager Sean Dyche wasn't afraid to play with two strikers in a hardworking 4-4-2 formation, using Chris Wood and Ashley Barnes as his frontline. Joe Hart and Tom Heaton competed for the keeper's jersey and Johann Gudmundsson, Ashley Westwood and Jack Cork were charged with creating chances from midfield. James Tarkowski and Ben Mee were reliable at the back and youngster Dwight McNeil enjoyed a breakthrough year.

SEASON STATS

POSITION:	15TH
PREMIER LEAGUE POINTS:	40
PREMIER LEAGUE WINS:	11
PREMIER LEAGUE GOALS SCORED:	45
PREMIER LEAGUE GOALS CONCEDED:	68
CLEAN SHEETS:	8
SHOTS:	360
PENALTIES SCORED:	2
PASSES:	13,011
CROSSES:	693
TACKLES:	583
YELLOW CARDS:	75
RED CARDS:	1
FOULS:	172
OFFSIDE:	106

MEGA MOMENT >

A 1–0 win over Champions League-chasing Spurs in February sent the fans wild. The result also set a new Premier League record for Burnley, as they went eight games without defeat for the first time. On the back of three straight defeats around Christmas, this was a much-needed record for the Burnley boys!

5 EPIC STARS

CHRIS WOOD
Whether starting or making an impact from the bench, Wood put pressure on defenders with his strength and heading. He scored ten goals in 2018–19.

ASHLEY WESTWOOD
Westwood hit top gear in the second half of the season. He's a tough midfielder who loves chasing, tackling and setting up strikers. He made seven assists.

JAMES TARKOWSKI
Burnley's top centre-back made 71 tackles, 235 clearances and scored a huge winner against Brighton & Hove Albion at Turf Moor in December.

JOHANN GUDMUNDSSON
The ice-cool Iceland star was involved in nine Premier League goals and made 491 passes from midfield. An impact substitute, too.

DWIGHT McNEIL
The eye-catching winger enjoyed a great run in the team from December to help Burnley set a club record eight games unbeaten.

PLAYER OF THE YEAR

ASHLEY BARNES

Barnes was Burnley's top scorer, sticking away 12 goals. His form from January to early March saw him strike six in nine games, including four in a row. Barnes has power, precision, an alert footy brain and the skills to score with either foot and from the penalty spot. A fantastic team player who never gives up for The Clarets.

POSITION:	FORWARD
PREMIER LEAGUE GAMES:	37
PREMIER LEAGUE GOALS:	12
PASSES:	518
ASSISTS:	2
CROSSES:	6
RIGHT-FOOT GOALS:	9
LEFT-FOOT GOALS:	1
YELLOW CARDS:	8
RED CARDS:	0
FOULS:	54

SOUTHAMPTON

TEAM TALK

Using three centre-backs and getting width from stars such as Valery and Bertrand, Southampton's well-drilled system and tactics really got the most out of their squad. Redmond sometimes supported main striker Ings, with Long and Austin useful additions from the bench. Alex McCarthy and Angus Gunn competed to become the club's first-choice keeper.

POSITION: 16TH
PREMIER LEAGUE POINTS: 39
PREMIER LEAGUE WINS: 12
PREMIER LEAGUE GOALS SCORED: 45
PREMIER LEAGUE GOALS CONCEDED: 65
CLEAN SHEETS: 7
SHOTS: 483
PENALTIES SCORED: 4
PASSES: 14,297
CROSSES: 664
TACKLES: 699
YELLOW CARDS: 71
RED CARDS: 3
FOULS: 217
OFFSIDE: 61

MEGA MOMENT >>>>>>

Although The Saints enjoyed their win over Arsenal, their 2–1 victory against another north London team was even better. On 9 March, Southampton grabbed three points from Spurs after coming back from behind for the first time in the season. Valery and Ward-Prowse both beat World Cup-winning keeper Hugo Lloris late in the second half.

5 EPIC STARS

PIERRE-EMILE HOJBJERG
Made captain by Ralph Hasenhuttl, the rock-hard midfielder is a fans' hero! The Dane collected seven yellow and two red cards.

JAN BEDNAREK
A key man in wins over Arsenal and Spurs, the defender linked up superbly with players such as Vestergaard, Yoshida and Stephens at the back.

NATHAN REDMOND
The exciting winger came to life in the second half of the season. He notched up six goals, four assists and made an average of almost 30 passes per match.

DANNY INGS
On loan from Liverpool FC, the striker had injuries but his goals helped to earn points against Crystal Palace, Brighton & Hove Albion, Arsenal and Huddersfield Town.

RYAN BERTRAND
Southampton were happy to see the left-back return to the team in February after injury. He gave the team a speedy attacking outlet down the wing.

PLAYER OF THE YEAR

JAMES WARD-PROWSE

The crowd-pleasing midfielder saw his value rocket again in 2019. His influence on games increases every season and boss Ralph Hasenhuttl describes his free-kick technique as "incredible." Ward-Prowse scored free-kicks against Manchester United and Tottenham Hotspur and finished with seven goals, 145 crosses and 720 passes!

POSITION:	MIDFIELDER
PREMIER LEAGUE GAMES:	26
PREMIER LEAGUE GOALS:	7
PASSES:	720
ASSISTS:	0
CROSSES:	145
RIGHT-FOOT GOALS:	6
LEFT-FOOT GOALS:	1
YELLOW CARDS:	4
RED CARDS:	0
FOULS:	22

Spain's La Liga was packed with awesome action in 2018–19! Check out the top four teams and biggest stars.

MESSI'S MEN STRIKE AGAIN!

BARCELONA

No one could stop the mighty Barcelona sweeping up their 26th La Liga title and seventh this decade. Messi and Luis Suarez mesmerized up front, scoring 57 between them in the league as Barca lost just three games all season. Ousmane Dembele and Philippe Coutinho began to repay their mighty price tags in attack and Gerard Pique patrolled the backline with his cool skills and power.

Count my league titles – all ten of 'em!

SEASON STATS

CHAMPIONS: BARCELONA
TOP SCORER: LIONEL MESSI (BARCELONA) 36 GOALS
PLAYER OF THE SEASON: LIONEL MESSI (BARCELONA)
BEST YOUNG PLAYER: SAMUEL CHUKWUEZE (VILLARREAL)
SURPRISE TEAM: GETAFE

Messi scored his **50th** hat-trick and **650th** goal in a 4–2 win at Sevilla in February 2019!

ATLETICO MADRID

Atletico took great delight in finishing higher than rivals Real Madrid for the second season in a row. Diego Simeone's team relied on the goals and assists of France striker Antoine Griezmann, who sadly left in the summer, with Alvaro Morata finding the net on loan from Chelsea. Experienced defender Diego Godin helped give Atletico the tightest defence in La Liga before he waved goodbye too.

REAL MADRID

VALENCIA

Getafe lost fourth place, and La Liga's final Champions League spot, on the last day of the season thanks to a 2–2 draw with Villarreal. Valencia ended with a 2–0 win over Real Valladolid. Rodrigo Moreno and Daniel Parejo were the only two to hit double figures for goals in the league as Valencia became the draw specialists in Spain.

Legendary manager Zinedine Zidane returned in March, after Real dramatically crashed out of the Champions League to Ajax. Striker Karim Benzema regularly got on the score sheet, hitting 21 in the league, and teenage Brazil forward Vinicius Junior showed signs of the sick talent he has too.

CELTIC'S GREAT EIGHT!

The Glasgow club stormed to their eighth league title in a row, holding off the challenge of city rivals Rangers. Here are the stats and stories from another super season in Scotland.

My goals were priceless!

CELTIC

Celtic wrapped up the championship in style, with manager Neil Lennon taking over from Brendan Rodgers in February. Striker Odsonne Edouard impressed, scoring 15 goals, and James Forrest, Scott Sinclair and Ryan Christie regularly hit the net. Keeper Scott Bain kept stacks of clean sheets in 2019 and Kieran Tierney, Kristoffer Ajer, Filip Benkovic, Mikael Lustig and ex-defender Dedryck Boyata helped to form a rock-hard defence.

SEASON STATS

CHAMPIONS: CELTIC
PREMIERSHIP TOP SCORER: ALFREDO MORELOS (RANGERS) 18 GOALS
PLAYER OF THE SEASON: JAMES FORREST (CELTIC)
BEST YOUNG PLAYER: ODSONNE EDOUARD (CELTIC)
SURPRISE TEAM: KILMARNOCK

RANGERS

Boss Steven Gerrard battled to get the better of Celtic in his first Premiership season. Morelos was his top scorer with 18 goals in the league and captain James Tavernier again did the business at right-back, chipping in with 14 strikes. Winger Ryan Kent caught the eye on loan from Liverpool FC.

Don't forget my 14 assists!

KILMARNOCK

Killie enjoyed a fabulous run at the start of the season and kept pace with the Glasgow clubs heading into Christmas. The highlight was their injury-time 2–1 win over the champions. Sadly their form dropped off and they slipped from the top two, but the likes of Greg Taylor, Eamonn Brophy, Gary Dicker and Alan Power can be very pleased with their season.

ABERDEEN

The Dons slipped two places from their 2018 finish, ending up behind Kilmarnock in fourth. Youngsters Lewis Ferguson, Sam Cosgrove and Scott McKenna were big stars for manager Derek McInnes. Cosgrove and Ferguson both netted in a dramatic 4–3 defeat at home to Celtic on Boxing Day!

HIGH-FLYING CANARIES!

Norwich City flew away with the Championship title! Let's take a look at how their promotion push took shape.

City were on the ball all season!

TRIPLE THREAT

Norwich City, Leeds United and Sheffield United battled it out for top spot for most of the season, with the boys from Norfolk holding off the threat from the two Yorkshire clubs. The three-way fight meant Norwich City had to keep grinding out results and picking up points right to the end!

BRILLIANT BOSS

Daniel Farke took a season to settle at Carrow Road, but his second campaign was one of the club's most exciting! He turned Norwich City into a formidable attacking force as they finished top scorers with 93 goals. The fans love him and he's made players like Emiliano Buendia, Onel Hernandez and Marco Stiepermann big stars.

COMEBACK KINGS

Nowich's never-say-die attitude sums up their amazing team spirit and hard work. They came from behind to beat teams such as Nottingham Forest, Aston Villa, Rotherham United, Bristol City and Millwall. The Canaries cracked in late goals too – Mario Vrancic's 97th-minute free-kick rescued a dramatic draw against Sheffield Wednesday!

YOUNG HEROES

Watch out for impressive defenders Jamal Lewis and Max Aarons. These eye-catching young full-backs were named in the PFA Championship Team of the Year after ripping it up all season. Attacking midfielder Buendia only turns 23 on Christmas Day and Todd Cantwell and Ben Godfrey are two more talented youngsters with big futures.

RANGERS

Boss Steven Gerrard battled to get the better of Celtic in his first Premiership season. Morelos was his top scorer with 18 goals in the league and captain James Tavernier again did the business at right-back, chipping in with 14 strikes. Winger Ryan Kent caught the eye on loan from Liverpool FC.

Don't forget my 14 assists!

KILMARNOCK

Killie enjoyed a fabulous run at the start of the season and kept pace with the Glasgow clubs heading into Christmas. The highlight was their injury-time 2–1 win over the champions. Sadly their form dropped off and they slipped from the top two, but the likes of Greg Taylor, Eamonn Brophy, Gary Dicker and Alan Power can be very pleased with their season.

ABERDEEN

The Dons slipped two places from their 2018 finish, ending up behind Kilmarnock in fourth. Youngsters Lewis Ferguson, Sam Cosgrove and Scott McKenna were big stars for manager Derek McInnes. Cosgrove and Ferguson both netted in a dramatic 4–3 defeat at home to Celtic on Boxing Day!

HIGH-FLYING CANARIES!

Norwich City flew away with the Championship title! Let's take a look at how their promotion push took shape.

City were on the ball all season!

TRIPLE THREAT

Norwich City, Leeds United and Sheffield United battled it out for top spot for most of the season, with the boys from Norfolk holding off the threat from the two Yorkshire clubs. The three-way fight meant Norwich City had to keep grinding out results and picking up points right to the end!

BRILLIANT BOSS

Daniel Farke took a season to settle at Carrow Road, but his second campaign was one of the club's most exciting! He turned Norwich City into a formidable attacking force as they finished top scorers with 93 goals. The fans love him and he's made players like Emiliano Buendia, Onel Hernandez and Marco Stiepermann big stars.

COMEBACK KINGS

Nowich's never-say-die attitude sums up their amazing team spirit and hard work. They came from behind to beat teams such as Nottingham Forest, Aston Villa, Rotherham United, Bristol City and Millwall. The Canaries cracked in late goals too – Mario Vrancic's 97th-minute free-kick rescued a dramatic draw against Sheffield Wednesday!

YOUNG HEROES

Watch out for impressive defenders Jamal Lewis and Max Aarons. These eye-catching young full-backs were named in the PFA Championship Team of the Year after ripping it up all season. Attacking midfielder Buendia only turns 23 on Christmas Day and Todd Cantwell and Ben Godfrey are two more talented youngsters with big futures.

TOP TEEMU

Striker Teemu Pukki had scored a handful of goals for clubs like Celtic and Schalke in his career, but the Finland forward absolutely smashed it for The Canaries! Pukki struck 29 in the league to land the golden boot and blast Norwich to the Championship crown.

Pukki is one of Norwich's best buys of all time – he was signed on a bargain **free transfer!**

Before winning promotion, **Sheffield United** were last in the Premier League in 2006–07!

THE BLADES RIP IT UP!

I put in some golden performances!

SHEFFIELD UNITED

The Blades lost just twice in the league in 2019 as their promotion push took them past Yorkshire rivals Leeds United. Chris Wilder's team had the class of David McGoldrick and Billy Sharp in attack, Oliver Norwood and John Fleck bossing midfield and Dean Henderson an ever present in goal. Second place was virtually clinched with a win over Ipswich Town on 27th April, but a narrow 1–0 win at Leeds in March was a huge boost!

SEASON STATS

CHAMPIONS: NORWICH CITY

CHAMPIONSHIP TOP SCORER: TEEMU PUKKI (NORWICH) 29 GOALS

PLAYER OF THE SEASON: TEEMU PUKKI (NORWICH CITY)

BEST YOUNG PLAYER: MAX AARONS (NORWICH CITY)

SURPRISE TEAM: SHEFFIELD UNITED

ASTON VILLA

Aston Villa were the form team going into the play-offs, winning ten games in a row to set up a semi-final with West Bromwich Albion. After beating The Baggies, Villa saw off Derby County at Wembley to seal a Premier League return. On-loan striker Tammy Abraham struck 26 goals in a memorable season.

DERBY COUNTY

After Derby County's sixth-place finish, they reached the play-off finals only to be beaten by Aston Villa. Midfielder Harry Wilson and strikers Martyn Waghorn and Jack Marriott grabbed the goals. Mason Mount, on loan from Chelsea, looked a class act in the middle of the pitch and was included in the England squad for the first time.

LEEDS UNITED

Leeds United fans were devastated not to secure automatic promotion, losing five of their last nine regular-season games to finish third. Derby County then knocked them out of the Championship play-off semi-finals. Kemar Roofe, Pablo Hernandez, Patrick Bamford and Mateusz Klich grabbed the goals for Bielsa's side throughout their exciting campaign.

These Premier League heroes need your help – some letters have been washed off their shirts! Under each player, write down what the name on each shirt should read.

MISSING LETTERS

I'm a champion at quizzes!

①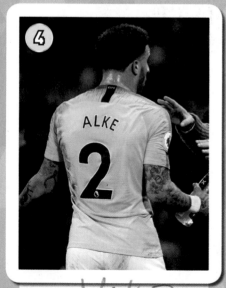
RIC
41

ANSWER: Re'Ce

②
CHIL L
3

ANSWER: chiliqhiL

③
I KS
8

ANSWER: Winks

④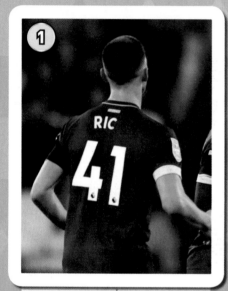
ALKE
2

ANSWER: WALKE

⑤
LACA E
9

ANSWER: LaKCAZet

⑥
RA FORD
10

ANSWER: RashFort

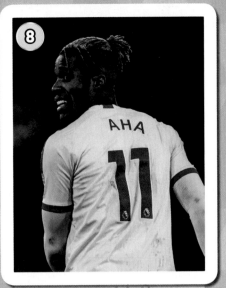

7

ALE NDER-ARN

66

ANSWER: Alex-rrnder

8

AHA

11

ANSWER: Zaha

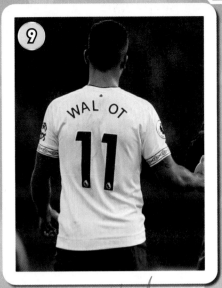

9

WAL OT

11

ANSWER: Walkot

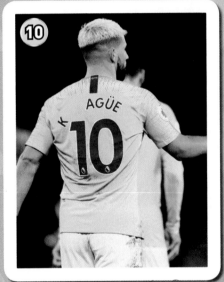

10

AGÜE

10

ANSWER: AGUEB

11

EENEY

9

ANSWER: ROeeny

12

ONDO

9

ANSWER: RonNDo

13

MOO

10

ANSWER: MOOY

14

I UAIN

9

ANSWER: HiGUAiN

15

LA ELA

11

ANSWER: Lamela

ANSWERS ON PAGE 79.

BAYERN BAG IT AGAIN!

The title race in Germany went to the final match day, with Bayern Munich and Borussia Dortmund competing for the silverware! Read on to reveal what happened.

BAYERN MUNICH

Surprise defeats to Hertha Berlin and Borussia Monchengladbach saw Bayern drop to fifth in the table early on. The serial champions bounced back, though, and a 5–0 win over Borussia Dortmund in April put them in pole position. Robert Lewandowski was a menace as usual, blasting 22 goals, with Serge Gnabry, Thomas Muller, Leon Goretzka and James Rodriguez chipping in too. It was Bayern's 28th Bundesliga title and their seventh in a row!

Lewandowski has an incredible scoring record for Bayern, netting **191** goals in **242** games.

SEASON STATS

CHAMPIONS: BAYERN MUNICH

BUNDESLIGA TOP SCORER: ROBERT LEWANDOWSKI (BAYERN MUNICH) 22 GOALS

PLAYER OF THE SEASON: LUKA JOVIC (EINTRACHT FRANKFURT)

BEST YOUNG PLAYER: JADON SANCHO (BORUSSIA DORTMUND)

SURPRISE TEAM: EINTRACHT FRANKFURT

Catch me if you can!

BORUSSIA DORTMUND

Dortmund came so close to their first title since 2012! Spanish star Paco Alcacer ripped defenders apart all season, scoring 18 goals and having a knack for hitting important late strikes. Marco Reus was another reliable scorer and Jadon Sancho reached 26 goals and assists combined. The winger also made his England debut to become the hottest property in the Bundesliga.

Sancho left Manchester City for Dortmund in summer 2017 and now bosses the Bundesliga!

RB LEIPZIG

Goal machines Timo Werner and Yussuf Poulsen fired Ralf Rangnick's RB Leipzig into a Champions League spot. The team really stepped up a gear in 2019, stretching an unbeaten league run to 15 games and getting six wins in a row in April. Marcel Halstenberg, Lukas Klostermann, Willi Orban and Marcel Sabitzer were some of the star men.

BAYER LEVERKUSEN

Peter Bosz's Leverkusen held off the challenge from Borussia Monchengladbach, Wolfsburg, Eintracht Frankfurt and Werder Bremen for the final Champions League spot. A 6–1 thrashing of Frankfurt in May, where they scored all six in the first half, put them on track for top-level European football in 2019–20.

BRIGHTON & HOVE ALBION

TEAM TALK

With players such as March, Knockaert and Izquierdo, Brighton & Hove Albion often attacked down the wings to get crosses over for Murray and Andone. Duffy and Dunk helped to keep their defence tighter than the likes of Burnley, Southampton, Cardiff City and Fulham in the table around them. Three 1–0 wins in a row in October gave the team a massive boost.

SEASON STATS

POSITION: 17TH
PREMIER LEAGUE POINTS: 36
PREMIER LEAGUE WINS: 9
PREMIER LEAGUE GOALS SCORED: 35
PREMIER LEAGUE GOALS CONCEDED: 60
CLEAN SHEETS: 7
SHOTS: 371
PENALTIES SCORED: 5
PASSES: 14,109
CROSSES: 636
TACKLES: 681
YELLOW CARDS: 60
RED CARDS: 4
FOULS: 235
OFFSIDE: 90

MEGA MOMENT > > > > > >

The win over Manchester United was epic, but the fans loved beating rivals Crystal Palace 3–1 in December even more! In a crazy game at the Amex Stadium, The Seagulls played with ten men for 62 minutes but were 3–0 ahead at the break. Leon Balogun and Florin Andone bagged beauties as Brighton & Hove Albion made it six wins from 15 matches.

5 EPIC STARS

SHANE DUFFY
Tackles, blocks, headers, interceptions – Duffy bossed the backline and also bagged five goals as Brighton & Hove Albion beat the drop!

ANTHONY KNOCKAERT
The Frenchman was the team's creative star, scoring twice, setting up six goals in 2018–19 and making 107 crosses. Slick!

LEWIS DUNK
The no-nonsense centre-back played in all but two games for the club. Dunk made 42 tackles, 118 headed clearances and hit the net against Everton and Cardiff.

FLORIN ANDONE
Playing in a 'super sub' role, the striker scored a vital headed winner against Huddersfield Town after coming off the bench. A handful for defenders.

SOLLY MARCH
The hardworking left-winger marched on in 2018–19, making five assists and scoring once for The Seagulls. He missed just three games over the whole season.

Murray scored in league victories at home and away against his old club **Crystal Palace** last season!

Murray has been mint again!

PLAYER OF THE YEAR

GLENN MURRAY

Murray's goals did so much to keep the club out of the bottom three. The powerful striker netted in wins over Manchester United, West Ham United, Wolverhampton Wanderers, Crystal Palace and Fulham. He's awesome in the air and deadly from the penalty spot, and even though Murray turns 36 in 2019, he's still a force in front of goal!

POSITION:	STRIKER
PREMIER LEAGUE GAMES:	38
PREMIER LEAGUE GOALS:	13
PASSES:	606
ASSISTS:	1
CROSSES:	8
RIGHT-FOOT GOALS:	10
LEFT-FOOT GOALS:	1
YELLOW CARDS:	5
RED CARDS:	0
FOULS:	80

Cardiff City fans loved their rollercoaster Premier League ride, even though it finished with the club sliding out of the division. Take a journey back over their season.

CARDIFF CITY

TEAM TALK

The Bluebirds battled like warriors for Premier League survival. Neil Warnock's game plan demanded a strong defence, long balls forward and tackling and chasing the opposition all over the pitch. Cardiff worked hard until the final whistle and Kenneth Zohore, Victor Camarasa and Sol Bamba all grabbed incredible 90th-minute winners in 2018–19!

POSITION: 18TH	
PREMIER LEAGUE POINTS: 34	
PREMIER LEAGUE WINS: 10	
PREMIER LEAGUE GOALS SCORED: 34	
PREMIER LEAGUE GOALS CONCEDED: 69	
CLEAN SHEETS: 10	
SHOTS: 417	
PENALTIES SCORED: 3	
PASSES: 10,226	
CROSSES: 562	
TACKLES: 655	
YELLOW CARDS: 66	
RED CARDS: 1	
FOULS: 196	
OFFSIDE: 77	

MEGA MOMENT > > > > > >

Beating AFC Bournemouth 2–0 in February gave Cardiff City their first win of 2019, but it was also an emotional victory for the club. It was their first home game since new striker Emiliano Sala sadly died and fans at the Cardiff City Stadium paid their respects to the Argentine. Bobby Reid's double gave The Bluebirds all three points.

5 EPIC STARS

SOL BAMBA
With 175 clearances, 74 tackles, seven clean sheets and four goals, it was a huge blow when Bamba's season ended in March because of injury.

CALLUM PATERSON
Can play in defence or midfield, but in 2018–19 he mainly operated in attack and scored goals against Southampton, Brighton & Hove Albion and Fulham.

ARON GUNNARSSON
Cardiff's crunching midfielder is a defensive star. He protects The Bluebirds' back four and clocked up an impressive 749 passes last season in the Premier League.

HARRY ARTER
In defence or attack, Arter was an influential midfielder in 2018–19. He made 62 tackles and picked up ten yellow cards. He's a tough opponent!

VICTOR CAMARASA
On loan from La Liga club Real Betis, the Spaniard chipped in with five goals and four assists. A tidy and creative midfielder with a fabulous right foot.

PLAYER OF THE YEAR

NEIL ETHERIDGE

From penalty saves to punching, catching and accurate distributions, Etheridge had a fantastic first Premier League season. He played in every league game and recorded clean sheets against the likes of Leicester City and Manchester United. The keeper controlled his box and his centre-backs knew they could rely on his super reflexes.

POSITION:	GOALKEEPER
PREMIER LEAGUE GAMES:	38
CLEAN SHEETS:	10
GOALS CONCEDED:	69
SAVES:	141
PENALTIES SAVED:	3
PUNCHES:	11
CATCHES:	6
YELLOW CARDS:	2
RED CARDS:	0
FOULS:	0

FULHAM

> I've got a Craven for goals!

TEAM TALK

After just one win in their first 12 league outings, Fulham knew they had to be much tougher at the back. They picked up wins over Southampton, Huddersfield Town and Brighton & Hove Albion with Aleksandar Mitrovic's goals doing the damage. Fulham spent over £50 million on key players Alfie Mawson and Andre-Frank Zambo Anguissa, but injuries hit their season.

POSITION:	19TH
PREMIER LEAGUE POINTS:	26
PREMIER LEAGUE WINS:	7
PREMIER LEAGUE GOALS SCORED:	34
PREMIER LEAGUE GOALS CONCEDED:	81
CLEAN SHEETS:	5
SHOTS:	454
PENALTIES SCORED:	2
PASSES:	17,699
CROSSES:	611
TACKLES:	591
YELLOW CARDS:	68
RED CARDS:	2
FOULS:	209
OFFSIDE:	90

MEGA MOMENT >>>>>

Fulham's exciting 3–2 win over Southampton was Claudio Ranieri's first game as manager before later being replaced by Scott Parker. It ended their run of six league losses in a row and gave the crowd hope they could escape the relegation zone. Their first clean sheet of the campaign, away at Newcastle United, was also one for the fans to cheer.

5 EPIC STARS

ANDRE SCHURRLE
The German World Cup winner brought class to Fulham's midfield. Schurrle got six goals, made 523 passes and 41 crosses into the box for the attackers.

CALUM CHAMBERS
Chambers enjoyed his new role as a defensive midfielder. In 2018–19 the ex-Arsenal man notched up 63 tackles and completed 1,484 passes.

RYAN SESSEGNON
The teenager's first Premier League season was full of exciting skills and hard work. The midfielder was involved in eight goals for Fulham in total.

JEAN MICHAEL SERI
The combative midfielder was a busy boy between the boxes. He won the official Premier League goal of the month in August for his strike against Burnley!

TOM CAIRNEY
The Cottagers' captain worked tirelessly in Fulham's effort to beat the drop. Cairney made 58 accurate long balls and won 129 duels in defence.

Mitrovic might think he's an unlucky player – he hit the woodwork three times in the Premier League last season!

PLAYER OF THE YEAR

ALEKSANDAR MITROVIC

There's no doubt who Fulham's danger man was last season! The powerful Serbia striker top scored with 11 goals in 37 appearances. Mitrovic buried six headers and scared defenders silly every time he leapt to meet a cross. He was well worth his reported transfer fee of £22 million in the summer of 2018.

POSITION:	STRIKER
PREMIER LEAGUE GAMES:	37
PREMIER LEAGUE GOALS:	11
PASSES:	1,026
ASSISTS:	3
CROSSES:	6
RIGHT-FOOT GOALS:	5
LEFT-FOOT GOALS:	0
YELLOW CARDS:	7
RED CARDS:	0
FOULS:	61

HUDDERSFIELD TOWN

TEAM TALK

Huddersfield Town struggled for goals in 2018–19, scoring just 22 times. David Wagner was replaced with Jan Siewert in January as the club tried to turn things around. Laurent Depoitre, Aaron Mooy, Alex Pritchard, Steve Mounie and new signing Karlan Grant were their threats going forward as Christopher Schindler and Terence Kongolo stayed busy in defence. Captain Tommy Smith was troubled by injury.

SEASON STATS

POSITION:	20TH
PREMIER LEAGUE POINTS:	16
PREMIER LEAGUE WINS:	3
PREMIER LEAGUE GOALS SCORED:	22
PREMIER LEAGUE GOALS CONCEDED:	76
CLEAN SHEETS:	5
SHOTS:	400
PENALTIES SCORED:	1
PASSES:	15,902
CROSSES:	769
TACKLES:	710
YELLOW CARDS:	55
RED CARDS:	4
FOULS:	232
OFFSIDE:	63

MEGA MOMENT > > > > >

Huddersfield Town's 2–0 win away to a quality Wolves side lifted them to 14th in the table. Mooy's double did the business and his second was a laser-guided free-kick past keeper Rui Patricio. The Terriers actually beat Wolves twice last season, picking up a fantastic 1–0 win in February after a last-gasp close-range strike by Mounie.

5 EPIC STARS

AARON MOOY
The creative Australian picked passes and threaded through balls. Mooy also had 43 shots and put 137 crosses into the box for The Terriers.

CHRISTOPHER SCHINDLER
The big German only missed one league game all season and his tackling, heading and interceptions were vital in central defence.

MATHIAS JORGENSEN
Known as Zanka, he was not only a key man at the back, but he also made an assist and scored against Leicester City, Brighton & Hove Albion and Manchester United.

STEVE MOUNIE
Mounie's main danger is his awesome aerial power. In 2018–19 he scored a sweet header against Burnley and also racked up three assists in the league.

JONATHAN HOGG
The popular defender won over 53 per cent of his tackles, made 72 defensive interceptions and won 31 aerial duels with the opposition.

At 193cm (6ft 6in), **Billing** is one of the tallest midfielders ever to appear in the Premier League!

Blingin' Billing is on the ball!

PLAYER OF THE YEAR

PHILIP BILLING

The stylish Denmark star added a physical side to his game in 2018–19 as Huddersfield Town competed for vital league points. Billing is a tall and elegant midfielder who averaged almost 40 passes per match and made 74 tackles during the season. His man-of-the-match display in the 2–0 win at Wolves alerted everyone to his top talent!

POSITION:	MIDFIELDER
PREMIER LEAGUE GAMES:	27
PREMIER LEAGUE GOALS:	2
PASSES:	1,074
ASSISTS:	0
CROSSES:	56
RIGHT-FOOT GOALS:	0
LEFT-FOOT GOALS:	1
YELLOW CARDS:	7
RED CARDS:	0
FOULS:	37

SPOT THE SPOT-KICK!

Blasting a penalty past the keeper isn't easy. Another tough task is guessing which ball in each of these pictures is the real one!

Ruben Neves **WOLVERHAMPTON WANDERERS v Everton**   THE REAL BALL IS: 3

Pierre-Emerick Aubameyang **ARSENAL v Tottenham Hotspur**   THE REAL BALL IS:

Matt Ritchie NEWCASTLE UNITED v Manchester City

THE REAL BALL IS: 2

Paul Pogba MANCHESTER UNITED v Young Boys

THE REAL BALL IS: 3

ANSWERS ON PAGE 79.

With Kylian Mbappe smashing in the goals, PSG captured the Ligue 1 title without breaking a sweat! Check out all the stats and facts from France...

BACK-TO-BACK CHAMPIONS!

PARIS SAINT-GERMAIN

With £200 million superstar Neymar out injured between January and April, World Cup winner Mbappe carried on his red-hot scoring form. He netted hat-tricks over Monaco and Guingamp, plus a four-goal haul against Lyon in October. Neymar and Edinson Cavani grabbed over 30 league goals between them and winger Angel Di Maria reached double figures for assists.

SEASON STATS

CHAMPIONS: PARIS SAINT-GERMAIN
LIGUE 1 TOP SCORER: KYLIAN MBAPPE (PSG) 33 GOALS
PLAYER OF THE SEASON: KYLIAN MBAPPE (PSG)
BEST YOUNG PLAYER: ISMAILA SARR (RENNES)
SURPRISE TEAM: REIMS

At just 20 years old, **Mbappe** is the youngest player to score **30** goals in a Ligue 1 season.

"Not a bad scoreline!"

LILLE

Lille's Ivory Coast striker Nicolas Pepe made headlines in 2018–19, scoring 22 goals as the club finished second. Forward Jonathan Bamba also impressed in the box and superkid Rafael Leao became known as Portugal's Mbappe. Lille couldn't stop PSG taking the title, but they enjoyed thrashing the champions 5–1 at home!

LYON

Former Manchester United winger Memphis Depay continued his fine form in France, scoring ten times and linking up well with forwards Nabil Fekir and Martin Terrier. Moussa Dembele settled well in his first season after joining from Celtic – his five goals in March helped cement Lyon's third-place finish.

SAINT-ETIENNE

Former Sunderland attacking midfielder Wahbi Khazri was St. Etienne's top scorer in the league, with 13 goals and six assists. Just one defeat in nine games between March 16th to May 18th kept Jean-Louis Gasset's team in fourth place, safely ahead of Montpellier and Marseille.

RONALDO ROCKETS TO THE TITLE!

Juventus landed their eighth Italian championship in a row after another top-class campaign.

JUVENTUS

With just four defeats and finishing a mega 11 points ahead of second-placed Napoli, Juve cruised to the Serie A crown in 2019. Cristiano Ronaldo cost a record £99 million, but he repaid that with 21 league goals and eight assists. Joao Cancelo, Mario Mandzukic, Alex Sandro, Paulo Dybala and Miralem Pjanic were regular star players throughout another trophy-packed season in Turin.

You can't stop Ron!

SEASON STATS

CHAMPIONS: JUVENTUS
SERIE A TOP SCORER: FABIO QUAGLIARELLA (SAMPDORIA) 26 GOALS
PLAYER OF THE SEASON: KRZYSZTOF PIATEK (AC MILAN)
BEST YOUNG PLAYER: FEDERICO CHIESA (FIORENTINA)
SURPRISE TEAM: ATALANTA

Cristiano Ronaldo became the first player to win the league title in Italy, Spain and England.

NAPOLI

Goalscorers Dries Mertens, Arkadiusz Milik and Lorenzo Insigne blasted 43 between them to shoot Napoli to another runners-up spot in Serie A. Club captain Marek Hamsik made a move to China, allowing new Spain star Fabian Ruiz to show off his skills in midfield. Centre-back Kalidou Koulibaly proved he's one of the best in Europe.

ATALANTA

Gian Piero Gasperini's awesome Atalanta team secured Champions League football for the first time after an amazing campaign. They finished third and were Serie A's top scorers with 77 goals. Colombian striker Duvan Zapata blasted 23 goals, while Josip Ilicic hit 12. A 3–1 win over Sassuolo on the final day kept them in the top three.

INTER MILAN

Star striker Mauro Icardi was much quieter in front of goal than the previous season, netting 11 in Serie A for Inter. Winger Ivan Perisic, midfielder Marcelo Brozovic and defender Milan Skriniar became key men in the team's spine. Watch out for Argentine goalscorer, Lautaro Martinez, who could develop into a deadly frontman for the Nerazzurri!

HATS OFF TO LUTON!

Luton Town and Barnsley took the top two spots in League 1, earning both teams a place in the Championship!

Luton Town dropped out of the football league altogether between 2009 and 2014!

LUTON TOWN

The Hatters wrapped up the title on the last day of the season thanks to a 3–1 win over Oxford United. Luton Town were the best team all season, losing only six games and finishing as top scorers with 90 goals. Striker James Collins took the golden boot with 25 strikes and ended the season by scoring in five games in a row. Elliot Lee, Jack Stacey and midfielder Pelly-Ruddock Mpanzu were vital stars as caretaker boss Mick Harford did a top job at Kenilworth Road.

SEASON STATS

CHAMPIONS: LUTON TOWN
LEAGUE 1 TOP SCORER: JAMES COLLINS (LUTON) 25 GOALS
PLAYER OF THE SEASON: AIDEN MCGEADY (SUNDERLAND)
BEST YOUNG PLAYER: JAMES JUSTIN (LUTON)
SURPRISE TEAM: DONCASTER

Championship, here we come!

BARNSLEY

The Tykes bounced straight back to the Championship, ending the season on an impressive 91 points and just seven losses. Keiffer Moore spearheaded their frontline, blasting 17 league goals despite a serious injury in February. Moore was named in the League 1 team of the season, along with his team-mates Dimitri Cavare, Ethan Pinnock, Adam Davies and Alex Mowatt.

CHARLTON ATHLETIC

The Addicks escaped League 1 after three years thanks to a dramatic play-off final win over Sunderland. They scored an injury-time winner through captain Patrick Bauer to secure a 2–1 victory and a spot in the Championship. Lyle Taylor led their attack and struck 33 goals and assists combined throughout the season.

SUNDERLAND

Former Premier League giants Sunderland suffered a League 1 play-off final defeat at Wembley, just eight weeks after losing the EFL Checkatrade Trophy final there. Experienced midfielder Aiden McGeady was The Black Cats' star man, hitting 12 goals and five assists. Youngster Josh Maja scored 15 goals before joining Bordeaux in January.

Lincoln ran away at the top of the table, with Bury and MK Dons holding on for automatic promotion!

Going up, going up, going up!

THE IMPS CLINCH CROWN!

LINCOLN CITY

Danny Cowley's well-drilled team were up as early as 13th April and pocketed the title nine days later. They had the second-best defence and attack in the division and stretched out a superb 19-game unbeaten run between late December and April. The Imps' defenders Neal Eardley, Jason Shackell and Harry Toffolo controlled it at the back, leaving striker John Akinde to cause damage with 15 goals and six assists.

SEASON STATS

CHAMPIONS: LINCOLN CITY

LEAGUE 2 TOP SCORER: JAMES NORWOOD (TRANMERE ROVERS) 29 GOALS

PLAYER OF THE SEASON: JAMES NORWOOD (TRANMERE ROVERS)

BEST YOUNG PLAYER: ARTHUR IONTTON (STEVENAGE)

SURPRISE TEAM: TRANMERE ROVERS

BURY

The Shakers know what it takes to clinch promotion to the third tier: this was the third time Bury had done it in the last nine seasons! Creative midfielders Danny Mayor and Jay O'Shea were the driving force for boss Ryan Rowe, with forward Nicky Maynard slotting in 21 goals from just 34 starts. A 14-game unbeaten run at the start of the year kept them in the race.

TRANMERE ROVERS

Tranmere Rovers sealed promotion the hard way, grabbing an extra-time winner to beat Newport County in the play-off final. Connor Jennings was the goal hero in that dramatic contest at Wembley. Striker James Norwood was in red-hot form, scoring 30 goals in all competitions to land the Golden Boot for Micky Mellon's men.

MK DONS

Powered by their 'Double A' strikeforce of Kieran Agard and Chuks Aneke, MK Dons sealed third spot with a dramatic 1–0 win over promotion rivals Mansfield Town on the very last day. Agard and Aneke smashed an epic 37 League 2 goals between them in 2018–19. Boss Paul Tisdale enjoyed his first season with The Dons, despite back-to-back defeats in April putting huge pressure on their challenge.

7 QUESTIONS ABOUT...
NUMBER 7S

MBAPPÉ

ooredoo

1 For which club did Alexis Sanchez play before he joined Manchester United?

ANSWER: *Arsenal*

2 Which England youngster wears the No.7 for German giants Borussia Dortmund?

ANSWER: *SANCHO*

My Korea at Spurs is really taking off!

3 Who's the France superstar bossing Chelsea's midfield in the No.7 shirt?

ANSWER: *Kanta*

4 Who wears the No.7 at Paris Saint-Germain – Neymar, Mbappe or Cavani?

ANSWER: *MBAPPE*

5 What nationality is Tottenham Hotspur's Son Heung-Min?

ANSWER: *South Korean*

6 Who became a new No.7 star for Juventus in 2018?

ANSWER: *Ronaldo*

7 Can you name the Barcelona No.7 who also played for Liverpool FC?

ANSWER: *Suarez*

ANSWERS ON PAGE 79.

LIVERPOOL FC

CHAMPIONS 2018-19

THE REDS RUL

Liverpool FC lifted the 2018–19 UEFA Champions League trophy after a thrilling win over Spurs!

1 How many times have Liverpool FC won the UEFA Champions League? Is it once, twice or six times?

ANSWER:

2 Which two players scored for The Reds in their 2–0 final win over Tottenham Hotspur?

ANSWER:

The current UEFA Champions League trophy stands at **73.5cm** tall and weighs **7.5kg**!

6 How many goals did The Reds' attacking trio of Salah, Mane and Firmino score in Europe in 2018–19? Was it three, 13 or 23?

ANSWER:

7 How many times have Tottenham Hotspur appeared in a UEFA Champions League final?

ANSWER:

3 In which Spanish city was the 2018–19 UEFA Champions League final played?

ANSWER:

4 Who lifted the trophy as captain of The Reds?

ANSWER:

5 Which team did Liverpool FC famously beat in the semi-finals?

ANSWER:

EUROPE!

8 Liverpool boss Jurgen Klopp had previously lost the final as manager of which German club?

ANSWER:

Third time lucky! Get in!

9 Which Tottenham Hotspur star scored a stunning hat-trick in the semi-finals to beat Ajax?

ANSWER:

10 Who had four assists in the tournament in 2018–19? Was it Alexander-Arnold, Mane or Shaqiri?

ANSWER:

ANSWERS ON PAGE 79.

SPOT THE DIFFERENCE

Circle the 10 differences between the two pictures.
Tick as you find them.